Festivals Around the World

Cameron Macintosh

Contents

Aboriginal and Torres Strait Islander peoples are advised that this text may contain the names and images of people who have passed away.

Fantastic Festivals

Festivals are a highlight of people's lives in many parts of the world. Festivals bring people together to celebrate important occasions. A festival can celebrate the achievements of a particular group of people or an event in nature, such as the beginning of a new season. Some festivals are held to celebrate a region's culture, including its art and music.

The Lunar New Year is celebrated in China with a dragon dance.

For Holi, the Hindu spring festival in India, people throw coloured water and powders over one another.

Festivals allow people to experience new things and meet new people they might not otherwise encounter in their daily lives. Most importantly, festivals are a lot of fun!

Matariki Festival, New Zealand

Matariki is the name for the **Māori** New Year in New Zealand (Aotearoa). Matariki takes place in May, June or July, when the Pleiades (pronounced *plee-ay-dees*) star cluster comes into view in the New Zealand sky in the early morning. Matariki is the Māori name for the Pleiades.

A Māori dance group (Te Wharekura o Hoani Waititi) performs at the 2017 Matariki festival.

The Pleiades star cluster is also known as the Seven Sisters. It appears to be made up of seven bright blue stars, but it actually contains more than 1000 stars.

The haka, a Māori dance performance, is often part of the Matariki Festival.

For Māori people, Matariki has long been a time for families and communities to come together and look back on the previous year. It is also a time to make plans for the year ahead.

Today, people of all backgrounds gather for Matariki to enjoy events that celebrate Māori culture, such as concerts and feasts. Matariki is a public holiday for all New Zealanders.

Lake Bolac Eel Festival (Kuyang Lapakira), Australia

Lake Bolac, in the state of Victoria, Australia, is a **sacred** site to the Wadawurrung, Girai wurrung and Djab wurrung peoples. For thousands of years, it was a gathering place during the eel migration season, in the months from March to May. At this time, large numbers of eels swam from the lake to the sea to have their young. They swam through rivers, shallow streams and swamps to reach the sea. This was a time of great significance for First Nations peoples. While they met at the lake to catch the eels, they also traded with each other and performed important ceremonies.

Kuyang Lapakira means "plenty of eels".

The southern shortfin eel is found in Lake Bolac.

Now, every second year, the First Nations peoples of the area welcome visitors to Lake Bolac to celebrate the eel season. Visitors to the Lake Bolac Eel Festival share in activities including performances by First Nations artists and workshops that teach visitors about local Aboriginal cultures.

At the Lake Bolac Eel Festival, there is a Twilight Ceremony with dance and storytelling performances.

This sculpture of a brolga was made for the Lake Bolac Eel Festival by local First Nations artists Bronwyn Razem and Dave Jones.

Yee Peng Lantern Festival, Thailand

Each November, when the Ping River in Chiang Mai, Thailand, is at its highest and the moon is full, the local people celebrate the Yee Peng Lantern Festival. During the festival, people release lanterns into the night sky. As they release their lanterns, they make wishes for the coming year and let go of anything bad that has happened in the previous year. Many people also decorate their homes with colourful flags and smaller lanterns.

People release lanterns into the sky at the Yee Peng Lantern Festival.

The festival attracts tourists from around the world. Apart from watching the lanterns rising into the sky, visitors to the festival can enjoy Thai food sold by street **vendors**. They can also watch traditional Thai dance performances, fireworks displays and a large street parade.

Most festival lanterns are made from a wooden or bamboo frame, wrapped in rice paper. A candle is placed inside. This makes the lantern rise into the sky like a hot-air balloon.

Thai children participate in the Lantern Festival.

A woman rides on a colourful float in the Yee Peng Lantern Festival street parade.

International Kite Festival, India

Each year, for a week in January, people come from all over India and around the world to enjoy the International Kite Festival in the city of Ahmedabad. The skies above the city are filled with colourful kites of all shapes and sizes. Some visitors to the festival join in the kite flying, while others are happy to simply watch and admire the kites in the sky.

The festival was first held in 1989 to celebrate Uttarayan (pronounced *oo-ta-rye-an*), the time of year when winter ends and food **harvesting** can begin.

People fly kites of all shapes and sizes at the International Kite Festival.

A boy flies a kite from the top of a mosque in Delhi, India.

The festival attracts skilled kite makers and kite fliers from around the world. Local people also make their own kites, using brightly coloured kite strings and bamboo frames. Families and neighbours then gather on the rooftops of the city buildings to fly their kites.

As well as kite flying, the festivities include special foods and performances, such as dancing and singing.

Some of the sculptures are colourfully **illuminated** at night. Visitors also enjoy the festive atmosphere, which includes food and drink vendors and live entertainment.

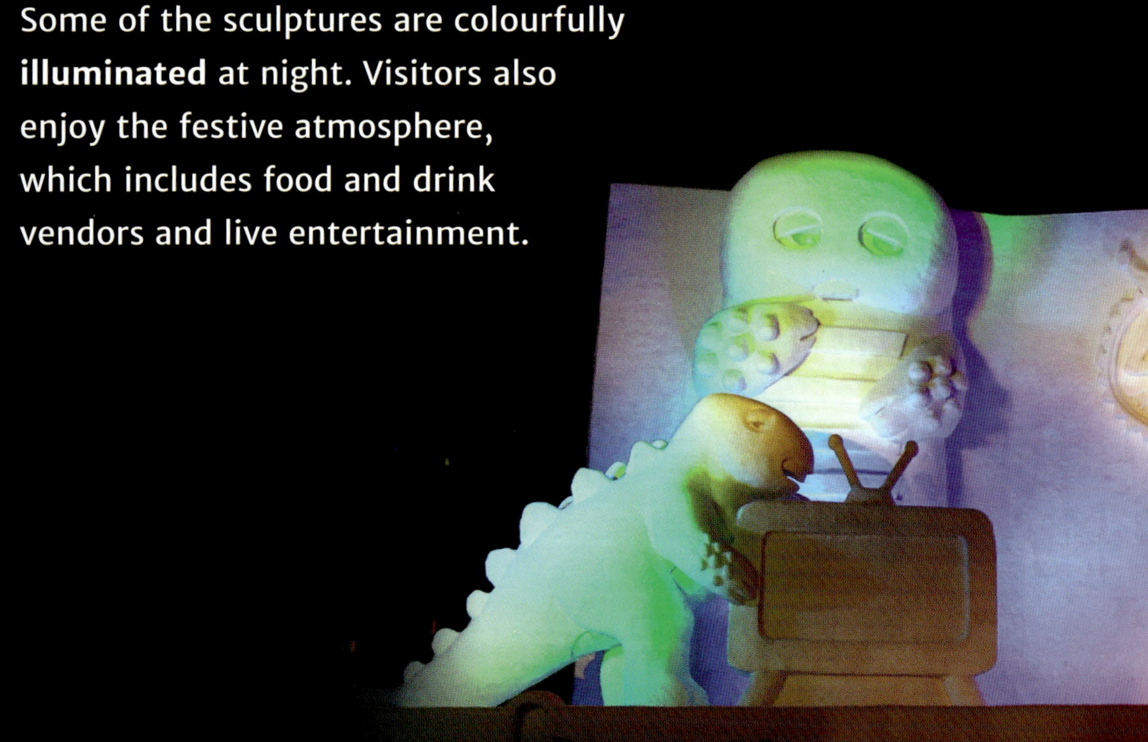

Colourful ice sculptures of popular movie and TV show characters light up the night sky.

An important part of the festival is the International Snow Sculpture Contest. Teams from countries around the world design and carve a sculpture from a block of ice. Spectators can watch from close by as each sculpture is created. Many of the sculptures tell a story or have a theme, such as protecting the environment or an endangered animal.

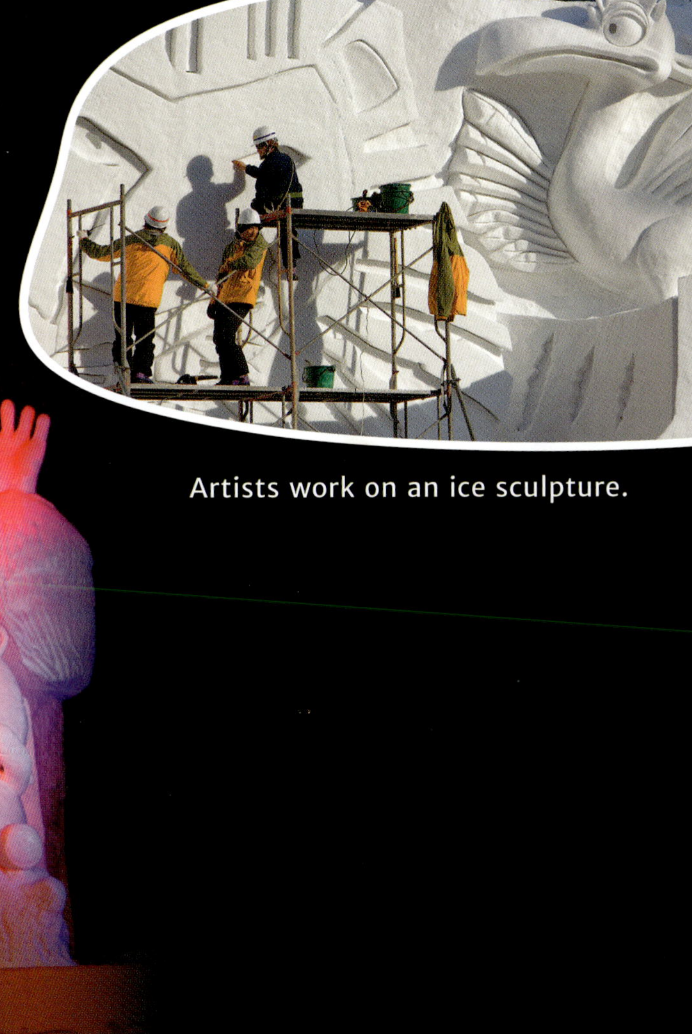

Artists work on an ice sculpture.

Panafest, Ghana

Panafest (the **Pan-African** Historical Theatre Festival) is a ten-day festival held every second year in Ghana. The festival celebrates the history and culture of the people of Ghana. It also celebrates the arts and cultures of other countries across the African continent.

Panafest was established in the 1980s. To begin with, it paid **tribute** to the many people of Africa who have been affected by **slavery**. Since then, the festival has continued to use theatre and other arts to entertain and educate audiences about many issues affecting the people of Africa.

A group of drummers perform at Panafest.

People from all nations are welcome at Panafest, but the festival particularly welcomes people of African background who were born overseas and have never been to Africa.

The festival features performances in music, dance, drama and poetry from leading performers and visual artists from all around the continent.

A Nigerian performer dances at Panafest.

Stilt walkers perform at Panafest.

Northern Lights Festival, Norway

The Northern Lights Festival is a music festival held in January or February each year in Tromsø (pronounced *trum-suh*), in northern Norway. Tromsø is a city built on two islands, surrounded by mountains and **fjords** (pronounced *fee-yords*).

The festival celebrates the aurora borealis, also known as the northern lights. The northern lights are brightly coloured streaks in the night sky, usually in shades of green and blue. They are visible in Tromsø between mid-September and April.

The northern lights appear in the sky over the city of Tromsø during the festival period.

During the festival, Tromsø becomes a city of music and dance – particularly jazz, classical music and opera. The festival includes a cruise on the waters of Tromsø, as well as art exhibitions and music classes.

The Northern Lights Festival first took place in 1988. It is now a ten-day festival, with well-known local and international musicians performing at indoor and outdoor concerts.

Pavement Spectacle, Austria

The Pavement Spectacle is a yearly street festival held over three days in July, in the city of Linz in Austria. Linz is well known for its art, music and museums.

The Pavement Spectacle began in 1987 as an event for street musicians, but it now also features jugglers, acrobats, dancers and other types of performers. Artists come from around the world to participate in the festival, which includes special events for children.

The official name for the Pavement Spectacle is a German word, "Pflasterspektakel", pronounced *fluss-ter-shpec-ta-kel.*

A fire dancer performs at the Pavement Spectacle.

Usually, more than 200 000 people attend the festival during its three days. It takes place in the city's main square and the streets around it, including Linz's main shopping street, Landstrasse (pronounced *lund-strusser*).

Acrobats perform for a crowd on the street.

A living statue blows a kiss.

Miming is another type of performance art at the Pavement Spectacle.

White Nights Festival, Russia

The White Nights Festival is a cultural event that features performers from all over Russia and around the world. The festival marks the beginning of summer in the city of St Petersburg, Russia, and usually runs from 11 June to 2 July.

The festival is named after the bright nights in St Petersburg. From late May to early July, the sun in St Petersburg never dips far below the **horizon**, so the night sky is lighter than usual.

The skies over Moscow stay lighter than usual from May to July.

The White Nights Festival provides many activities to make the most of the daylight. These include musical performances, ballet, theatrical **re-enactments** of historical events and even a marathon. One of the festival's highlights is the Scarlet Sails celebration, in which a tall ship floats along the Neva River with brightly lit scarlet sails, and fireworks light up the sky.

Children perform a dance for the White Nights Festival.

At the Scarlet Sails celebration, the ship's "scarlet sails" are inspired by a Russian fairy tale of the same name.

Flower Festival, Colombia

Each year since 1957, in late July or early August, the city of Medellin in Colombia comes together for their Flower Festival. Thousands of visitors also come to the festival, which celebrates the flowers that grow in **abundance** in Colombia.

The festival, which runs for ten days, features flower exhibitions and competitions as well as a wide range of cultural events, including parades, plays, concerts and a horse fair. The city is decorated with flowers, and many people make flower displays for their homes, too.

Two girls prepare flower arrangements for the Flower Festival.

The festival's main event is the Silleteros (pronounced *si-ye-teh-ros*) Parade. "Silleteros" is the name for the local flower growers. Hundreds of silleteros parade through the streets of Medellin, carrying flower arrangements on wooden frames on their backs. Their colourful displays are enjoyed by thousands of spectators.

Folk dancers perform onstage at the 2016 Flower Festival.

Silleteros carry their flower arrangements in the parade using a wooden frame on their back.

Red Earth Festival, USA

The Red Earth Festival, first held in 1987, is a celebration of the culture and art of the First Nations peoples of America. It takes place each year in June, in Oklahoma City. Native American people come from all over the USA to share their culture, including artworks and performances.

The festival provides an opportunity for people of all backgrounds to come together to deepen their understanding of Native American culture, art and history.

At the Red Earth Festival arts and crafts show, people can buy clay pottery and many other art items.

A Navajo girl wears a Native American costume.

The Red Earth Festival opens with a large parade through the streets of Oklahoma City, with Native American people from around the USA displaying their traditional clothing.

Artworks featured at the festival include painting, pottery, jewellery and sculpture. Visitors can also enjoy Native American dance performances and competitions.

The Fancy War Dance is a popular competition at the Red Earth Festival.

Festivals add colour and excitement to people's lives, and give them the chance to share their cultures and achievements with others. Festivals are important because they help people to learn about different histories and cultures, and about how people live, work and celebrate in different parts of the world.

Festivals, such as the Red Earth Festival, are a special experience to share with family and friends.

Two Days in the Sapporo Snow

By Frankie

Day One, 30 January

I was very excited to arrive this morning in the city of Sapporo, Japan! Mum, Ella and I are here to see the Sapporo Snow Festival, which begins tomorrow.

It's very cold here! There is snow everywhere, but as we stepped onto the street for the first time, I noticed that the footpaths were mostly free of ice and snow. Mum told me that this is because most of the footpaths here are heated.

The main reason we are here is to see the ice sculptures at Odori Park, in the middle of Sapporo. Odori Park is a huge, rectangular park surrounded by shops and buildings. We walked straight there to see if the sculptures were all ready for the festival tomorrow.

In the middle of the park, we could see artists putting the final touches on some very large ice sculptures, including one that looked like huge cartoon characters. Some of the sculptures had **scaffolding** around them, with people carving the ice several metres above the ground.

At the other end of the park, we saw people carving smaller blocks of ice using hand tools. A sign told us that these sculptures were part of a competition, with each sculpture being made by a team from a different country. One of the sculptures was a very **intricate** flower, and another was a miniature temple. It will be interesting to see how they all look when the festival begins tomorrow.

Day Two, 31 January

We spent this morning visiting galleries and art museums, but after lunch we went back to Odori Park. All of the scaffolds had been removed and we could see the incredible detail in the bigger sculptures. My favourite was a huge ice building that looked like a palace.

All of the competition sculptures we saw yesterday were now finished. We walked around and shared our opinions with each other about which sculpture deserved to win the top prize.

In the evening, we came back to Odori Park and saw the colourful lighting on the largest sculptures. It was absolutely spectacular. Some of them even had moving **projections** on them!

All around the edges of the park, small vans and cabins were selling food and drinks, and music was being played through large speakers.

The festival really feels like a big, snowy party. I hope we will come back next winter!

Glossary

abundance (*noun*)	a large amount of something
fjords (*noun*)	deep, narrow areas of sea between high cliffs
harvesting (*verb*)	gathering food that has been grown
horizon (*noun*)	the line where the sky appears to meet the surface of Earth
illuminated (*adjective*)	lit up
intricate (*adjective*)	finely detailed
Māori (*adjective*)	the First Peoples of New Zealand (Aotearoa)
pan-African (*adjective*)	including all people of African background
projections (*noun*)	pictures or videos shone onto a large surface
re-enactments (*noun*)	theatrical performances of events that happened in history
sacred (*adjective*)	important and highly respected within religious beliefs
scaffolding (*noun*)	a temporary structure around a large object that workers can stand on
slavery (*noun*)	the former practice of kidnapping people from their home countries and forcing them to work without pay

tribute (*noun*) a display of appreciation or respect

vendors (*noun*) people selling something

Index